The Great Frog Race

and Other Poems

by Kristine O'Connell George

Pictures by Kate Kiesler

With an Introduction by Myra Cohn Livingston

A TRUMPET CLUB SPECIAL EDITION

ISBN 0-590-68722-0

12 11 10 9 8 7 6 5 4 3 2 1 8 9/9 0 1 2 3/0

Printed in the U.S.A. 24

First Scholastic printing, September 1998

The illustrations for this book were executed in oil paint.
The text is set in 16/20-point Goudy.

The Great Frog Race

and Other Poems

For Courtney.
—*K. O. G.*

For Liza and her love of mud and polliwogs.
—*K. K.*

Introduction

I often think how particularly delightful it would have been to have known Kristine O'Connell George as a child. The poetry she brings to us from her past not only bespeaks a quiet, gentle appreciation and love of nature, but is also dented with nicks and scars that mark her as an occasional hoyden ready to engage in a rousing water fight, a willing accomplice for Zeke the thieving hound, and a rough and ready entrepreneur of "the great frog race." It isn't every young woman who can clearly observe ghost children "swinging in the moonlight . . . catching the moon between their knees" one minute, and the next soliloquize on the beauty of a grayed and dented metal bucket that "stays with its family / for life."

Kristine's poems are filled with surprises, those moments when the reader sees for the first time that a dragonfly, with "wings scored like windowpanes," is indeed a "tiny piece of flying / cellophane"; that "the porch light shines on rain / taking thin silken stitches / with strands of wet thread"; and that polliwogs are very like "chubby commas."

Hers is a world of the rugged western landscape, with its plowed fields, warm family ties, Canadian geese, monkey wrenches, and mended snow fences. It is a pragmatic world where mothers get lost on a Sunday drive, and one must, during music class, endure the ignominy of singing off key, but it is equally a delicate world where a spring wind, in silk skirts smelling of lavender, floats in to consume scones and tea before she rustles away, and a contrary star hides in the daisy bed. It is also a world of dreams, where a girl can climb up on a rent-a-nag and dream of "stallion and gallop / and wind in my hair," where there is the sensibility to smell air that is sharp and spicy like freshly sharpened pencils, and leisure to wait all summer for a weeping willow to weep.

In a time when we have a surfeit of verse whose purpose seems mainly to elicit a quick laugh, it is not only refreshing but urgent that our children hear poetry resonating with music, keen observation, fresh metaphor and personification, and meaningful flights of imagination. In *The Great Frog Race* and in books of poems to come, Kristine George promises us that!

—Myra Cohn Livingston

Polliwogs

Come see
What I found!
Chubby commas,
Mouths round,
Plump babies,
Stubby as toes.
Polliwogs!
Tadpoles!

Come see
What I found!
Frogs-in-waiting—
Huddled in puddles,
Snuggled in mud.

Plowed Fields

The plow carved furrows
Raked long deep lines
Straight as fork tines that
Stretch to the horizon
Rippling like fan spines
Of shadow and light.

Spring Wind

Smelling of lavender,
softly fluttering the curtains,
she looked inside,
then floated in
for tea and scones.

She sat in the wing chair,
long elegant fingers
tracing linen lilacs.

After tea
she whispered her thanks,
lifted her silk skirts,
and rustled away.

Rent-a-Horse

I dreamed of
stallion and gallop
and wind in my hair.

The stableman
didn't seem to care.
When I tried to ride
his old rent-a-nag,
I couldn't quite
get my legs down,
or my knees around.
I was stuck,
high off the ground,
so I sat, way up there,

and dreamed of
stallion and gallop
and wind in my hair.

Evening Rain

The porch light shines on rain
taking thin silken stitches
with strands of wet thread.
I run outside to the rain
to see what it is sewing.

Waterbugs

In the cement cistern
they are weaving,
drifting into evening's
shadows of lace.
Suddenly, they're late!

With quicksilver flicks
their whip-thin legs whisk
them away, leaving
only the narrow wakes
waterbugs make.

Tree Farm

We walk the long rows
of trees growing
in black plastic pots
and wooden boxes
until I spot
the perfect tree
different from the rest—
the one where a bird
has built her nest.

Come home, tree.
Come home, bird.
Come home with me.

Ghost Children

I hear the quiet clank of the chains
against the pole.
The ghost children are swinging
in the moonlight.
Warm breezes and spring smells float
on silvered grasses.
Ghost mothers creak the wicker rockers
on the porch
Talking softly as they weave their
honeysuckle crowns.
The children are swinging higher
into the trees
Catching the moon between their knees.

Meadow

A cloud of white gnats
hatching in the grass, swirling
a summer snowstorm.

Egg

There are
No tags, no tabs
Or wrapping paper,
Nor flaps, nor string,
Sticky tape or ribbon.
Never hidden up high
On a cupboard shelf.
Egg is a package
That can open
Itself.

Garden Hose

Our hose
dozes
in the
warm sun
and wonders

what to
be when it
grows up.

It imagines
fat black
irrigation pipe,
aqueducts,
transcontinental
pipelines.

We let
it have
its dreams.

Dragonfly

Hovering and darting,
brightly iridescent,
wings scored like windowpanes,
this tiny piece of flying
cellophane.

Metal Bucket

No one remembers when
(or even if)
they ever bought one.

One day, it's just there,
sharp and shiny
in the sun. Proud.

A thin strong handle,
lip rolled just so for pouring,
smooth flat bottom for sitting.

Later, grayed and dented,
it is even friendlier,
loyal and steadfast.

A metal bucket
stays with its family
for life.

What Happened to the Ice Cream Cone Someone Dropped

A crow stole the cone
and six tiny sparrows hopped
vanilla footprints
across the sidewalk.

Ambush

I threw
a small water balloon.
That's all.

I hid.
I tossed.
I ran.

My victim knows,
and lies in wait
with the garden hose.

The Great Frog Race

We used flashlights one night
to find them in the damp and secret
places in the garden.

We put the frogs in a cardboard box
and wet down the driveway.
The garden hose was the finish line.

One by one, we lined up the frogs.
(It wasn't easy.)
We yelled: *Ready– Set– Go!*

Seventeen frogs leaped in all directions,
croaking. *Blurk. Blurk. Blurk.*
The Great Frog Race was over quickly.

One by one,
all contestants hopped off
into the moonlight.

Sunday Drive with Mom

It's another Sunday drive—
just Mom and me, out for a spin.
Are we lost?

A winding road, and then
a curious turn—
Yes. We're lost.

Again.

Snow Fence

It's a sorry excuse for a fence:
Old pickets, branches, a broken plow
Lashed together with barbed wire and rope.
It runs midslope, leans downwind,
Pens nothing in, keeps nothing out.

Come summer, someone always mends it;
Adds something new, maybe a length of pipe
Or a table leg, whatever's handy.
Been there as long as I can remember,
Patient old fence,
Waiting for another November.

Zeke, an Old Farm Dog

The black dog on the knoll is my dog:
Sailing over construction fences,
Chasing bulldozers,
Barking at butterflies,
Swimming in the neighbor's
New backyard pool.

Now he steals things
And brings his prizes to the front porch:
Sunday papers and other dogs' pans,
Shingles, keys, someone's ham on rye.
I won't fence him in.
I won't even try.

SAM

Monkey Wrench

He jeers at me with a strong-jawed grin,
Juts out his wide silver chin—
Cranks the nuts tighter.
Biting stubborn rusted bolts,
Tackling hitches, engines, bikes,
No job's too big for him.
After a long hard day, monkey wrench
hangs upside down on his hook
above Dad's workbench,
                                        yawning.

Falling Star

Falling star,
Little star,
Skidding through space,
Won't go to bed.
Hides in the daisies
instead.

September

Sniff the air—
It smells
    Spicy. Sharp.
Like
    Freshly sharpened pencils.

Weeping Willow

I waited all summer
for my weeping willow
to weep. It sighed.

Its shoulders drooped
and branches sagged.
It never cried.

When autumn came
my willow wept
piles of tears for me to rake.

Quiddling with Words

I like words

like *Perforate*
that snap neatly
into brittle pieces
like a cracker,

like *Ricochet*
that spring madly
like a grasshopper
in a glass pickle jar,

like *Quiddle*
which I just discovered
in the dictionary
sandwiched between
Perforate and *Ricochet*.

Music Class

I hear birds. I sing frogs.
My heart hears every note,
yet my song is locked
inside my throat.
Someone laughs.
I'm way off-key.

The teacher holds my hand
and opens a special box
of things with secret voices.

I get maracas and triangle.
I am aria. I am madrigal.
With silver bells and tambourine,
        I can sing!

Canada Geese

Padded drum
of beating wings
fills the steel gray sky.
See them sketching, stretching skyward.
Hear their lonely cry. See them in the windswept
autumn. Hear them call
goodbye.

Morning Grasses

Thin frosted grasses
lying flat under footprints
slowly straighten up.

Winter Swing

The old wooden swing
hanging from the apple tree
is pillowed with snow.